INSIDER SECRETS TO

JEWELLERY BUYING

How Modern Buyers are Shopping smarter, not costlier

INSIDER SECRETS TO JEWELLERY BUYING

How Modern Buyers are Shopping smarter, not costlier

Rohan Siroya

Available on amazonkindle

Worldwide Published by

Pendown Press
PREMIUM BUSINESS PUBLISHER

PENDOWN PRESS LLP
An ISO 9001 & ISO 14001 Certified Co.,
Regd. Office: 3767A, Kanhaiya Nagar,
Tri Nagar, Delhi-110035
Ph.: 8130886000, 9650072927, 8595249536
E-mail: info@pendownpress.com
Branch Office: 1A/2A, 20, Hari Sadan, Ansari Road,
Daryaganj, New Delhi-110002
Ph.: 011-45794768
Website: PendownPress.com

Edition: 2025
Price: ₹ 1,199
ISBN: 978-81-9896-199-0

Layout and Cover Designed by Pendown Graphics Team
Printed and Bound in India by Thomson Press India Ltd.

Table of Contents

Section 3: Planning Like a Pro

Section 4: The Final Touch

Acknowledgements

This book was never a solo act, far from it. It's built on borrowed time, borrowed wisdom, and a lot of borrowed patience from the people around me.

To everyone who took time out of their packed lives to sit down and answer my endless questions — you probably didn't realize it then, but you were shaping this book more than I was. Your stories, your honesty, and your clarity helped me connect the dots I didn't even know existed. Without you, these pages would be empty, or worse, full of half-baked theories.

To the senior managers, the marketing minds, and the behind-the-scenes champions in my team — thank you for calling out my fluff, poking holes in my ideas, and helping me sharpen them into something usable. You kept me real. Mostly.

To Mr. Akshar Yadav and Mr. Rahul Jain — I owe you more than a line here. You've shifted how I think, how I lead, and how I make sense of this crazy journey. You've been part compass, part mirror.

A special shoutout to the salespeople on the frontlines — the ones who've made it their mission to serve, guide, and genuinely look out for customers. You've built trust one conversation at a time, offered honest advice when it mattered most, and created loyalty not with discounts, but with true value. The relationships you've quietly nurtured over the years form the foundation of why people connect with jewellery.

To my parents, my siblings, and my wife — you've seen the full circus. Thank you for nodding along even when you didn't fully get what I was chasing, and for backing me anyway. It means everything.

And lastly, to the unsung heroes of the jewellery world: the karigars. Your hands create what words can't. Your craft is the real poetry. If there's any beauty in these pages, it starts with you.

Thanks for being part of the madness.

Preface

The Secret Voice Inside Every Woman

Who This Book is For?

There's something timeless about jewellery.

In so many homes, be they Arab, Indian or almost anywhere in the world, a simple gold chain isn't just an accessory. It's a blessing from the elders. A security blanket tucked into a locker. A quiet reward after years of saving. Jewellery carries pride, protection, beauty, and most of all, emotion.

You don't walk into a jewellery store because you want a metal or a mineral.

You walk in because you want a feeling.

- Maybe it's the quiet pride of passing your gold bangles down to your daughter.
- Maybe it's the thrill of being noticed when you walk into a room.
- Or maybe the relief of knowing your money didn't just disappear into handbags and shoes, but into something that gleams and grows.

Jewellery is never just jewellery. It's proof –

- Of taste.
- Of success.
- Of smart choices.
- Of being remembered.

But here's the uncomfortable truth:

Thousands of women, educated, experienced, and well-travelled, walk out of jewellery stores every single day, holding a piece that doesn't quite feel right.

- The colour isn't what they expected.
- The shine fades too fast.
- The resale value? A disappointment.

Not because they didn't know what they liked. But because no one told them what to look for.

In an industry built on trust, the fine print is often invisible.

Let me tell you about a customer I met last year.

All That Glitters Isn't Worth It At Times

Let's call her **Ms.R** (*Name withheld for reasons of privacy). **A senior diplomat from Kuwait.** Smart. Independent.

She bought a diamond set at a prestigious exhibition. It looked perfect under showroom lights. But six months later, when she wore it to a wedding, something felt off.

The shine had dulled. The compliments never came as expected. She told me, **I spent all that money, and I'm still not sure I made the right choice.**

This book was born for women like her.

We saw smart, well-meaning buyers, especially women, still falling into the traps of

- Asking about gold rates, but not knowing when to buy.
- Misunderstanding "making charges."

- Believing "zero making charges" means zero tricks.
- Believing what the showroom lights tell them and forgetting to check what the certificate doesn't.
- Being misled about weights and terminology.
- Ending up buying jewellery that holds neither value nor emotion.

So we created this book.

Not to sell. But to serve.

From hundreds of quiet stories.

And from a louder truth:

Jewellery should never feel like a gamble.

This is your guide to buying with power, not pressure. To walk out of every store with something you'll wear, love, and never regret.

Because jewellery isn't just about buying. It's about becoming.

Becoming the woman who is remembered for –

- Her grace. For her wisdom.
- For her gold that told stories.
- For her diamonds that lit up a room.

Let's begin….

Why I'm Writing This Book

A Life Forged in Gold, Embellished With Diamonds

I grew up in a business family where the path was subtly laid out long before I ever took my first steps. In a home of overachievers, academic excellence was the currency of pride. My elder sister, sharp and diligent, always seemed to be one step ahead. My younger brother, driven and focused, soon surpassed me in scholarly pursuits. **I, however, was still figuring things out.**

I didn't know it at the time, but I was being shaped not by comparison, but by curiosity.

When the time came to step into the family jewellery business after university, I hesitated.

Not because I doubted the legacy, but because I hadn't yet found my identity within it.

So, in a moment of rebellion and self-searching, I moved to Mumbai.

There, I joined my uncle in the chaotic and unrelenting world of real estate, specifically in the wild west of slum rehabilitation projects. **It was Mumbai at its most raw:** legal grey zones, emotional negotiations, and the delicate dance of transforming chaos into order.

Four years of this taught me two things:

- First, how to survive under pressure

- Second, how cities like people often grow by breaking, then rebuilding.

Then came the turning point.

At the Indian School of Business, **a professor teaching 'Venture Capitalism' pushed me to think bigger. Much bigger. One conversation changed my career trajectory.**

I moved into uncharted waters, helming an over-the-counter pharma startup with multi-million-dollar backing from one of India's most respected media houses.

- We built it from scratch.
- We grew.
- We stumbled.
- We soared, then stumbled again.
- Then we exited.

A six-year rollercoaster left me with two priceless things:

The scars of experience, and a deep respect for scientific precision, something I now bring into every part of my life, including jewellery.

But an exit is never just a corporate event. For a founder, it can feel like heartbreak. And I did grieve.

I asked myself –

- Am I more capable now than I was before?
- Or just overly cautious?

That's when Dubai–my childhood home–called me back.

Coming Full Circle: Siroya Jewellers

My family business, **Siroya Jewellers**, was started long before Instagram reels and showroom lighting tricks. **For over 50 years,** our family has lived, breathed, and loved jewellery—not just as a business, but as a way to bring pride, protection, and purpose into people's lives.

Our journey began in the bustling bylanes of India and grew into one of the most respected gold and diamond houses in the Middle East. In the 1960s, my great-grandfather left the deserts of Rajasthan for the sweaty lanes of Zaveri Bazaar in Mumbai. A poor worker with calloused hands and a dream, he saved for years doing odd jobs before opening his first silver store. My grandfather and his brothers joined him, working 14-hour shifts by day and studying for law school under street lamps by night.

Then came the ban on silver exports—overnight, their business was gone. But not their spirit.

My grandfather's first job with a petroleum company took him to the Gulf. **In the barren beginnings of what we now call the UAE, he found hope. He partnered up with some old contacts and formed a company** in the real estate and jewellery business.

After parting ways with those partners, in 1992, he laid the foundations of what would become Siroya Jewellers along with his son and younger brother.

- My father and his uncle began by walking door to door—literally selling gold from briefcases.
- They built relationships before they built revenue.
- That trust became their currency.
- From 1992 to 1999, Siroya became one of the largest wholesale gold jewellery houses in the Middle East.
- By the 2000s, we opened our first retail showroom in Meena Bazaar, Bur Dubai. But then the aggressive expansion stopped.

- Our second store followed ten years later in the residential suburb of Al Qusais.

From Wholesale Giants to D2C Dreamers

Our wholesale business, exporting to 33 countries, has consistently earned us recognition as one of the largest gold importers in the world from India. That is our backbone. Our pride.

But I wanted to find my place in this legacy. Not just to inherit the crown, but to recast it.

- With a passion for storytelling, branding, and customer experience, **I ventured into lab-grown diamonds—a controversial and exciting space.**
- **We were the first in the GCC to position them within fine jewellery.** Many in the industry scoffed. Some ignored us. Others resisted.

But we saw what they didn't: a blue ocean waiting to be sailed.

Today, that sailboat is called **Evermore Diamonds**. **A D2C brand born not of tradition but of transformation.** Built on trust, driven by design, and deeply rooted in the idea that jewellery should be both expressive and ethical.

We've since then launched two new Siroya stores, taking the store count to four. Our philosophy is simple and broadly remains the same: treat every customer like family. Make every visit feel like home. Let jewellery be an experience, not a transaction.

Why This Book Had to Be Written

People think buying jewellery is about grams and rates. It's not. It's about gut and grace. It's about what you feel—when you hold a necklace, try on bangles, or see your reflection lit up by a diamond.

This book is a reflection of everything I've lived through: real estate slums, start-up storms, and showrooms shimmering with history.

Our family has served over 280000 retail customers. But that number means little if our knowledge stays locked in display cases and vaults.

I've written this to:

- Help you avoid the same mistakes I've seen even the smartest people make.
- Demystify a market that's often wrapped in deliberate confusion.
- Help you treat jewellery not as an impulse, but as an investment, for your soul and for your future.

This isn't theory. It's 50+ years of lessons passed down through generations, fused with my own modern-day experiences as a marketer, entrepreneur, and lifelong learner.

I've asked questions that made my mentors uncomfortable.

I've launched products others said wouldn't work.

I've listened more than I've spoken, and now, I'm ready to share.

So, who am I to write this book?

I'm the grandson of a dreamer, the son of a builder, and the founder of a brand that believes trust is the ultimate luxury.

I've been brash, been bold, and been blessed enough to serve in a business where emotion meets eternity.

If you're ready to make jewellery choices that last a lifetime—and pass down stories through sparkle—then you're exactly who this book was written for.

SECTION 1

Jewellery That Speaks to Your Soul

- Jewellery Is Never Just Jewellery
- Why emotions, not just prices, drive your decisions
- The Guardian & The Dreamer – Which One Are You?
- Gold for Legacy, Diamonds for Expression

A Question For You To Reflect On

What are you really buying this for?

Chapter 1

Jewellery is Never Just Jewellery

I get it, you are really busy.

But must you really walk into a jewellery store and, without pause or connection, point to a piece and ask, "How much?"

To me, that question misses the point entirely. You see, **I've always believed that we're not in the *product* business—we're in the *service* business.** And that changes everything.

Let me explain

Think back to a time when you visited a truly skilled hairdresser—perhaps tucked away in a salon you hadn't heard of before. As you stepped inside, something shifted. A soft, inviting fragrance floated through the air. A gentle breeze circulated perfectly, cooling the room just enough to make you want to stay. The floors had been freshly swept; you could almost smell the cleanliness, subtle hints of antibacterial freshness that reassured you without saying a word.

Then the music began—not loud or jarring, but a carefully curated playlist that matched your mood, transporting you away from the chaos of the street outside and into a space that felt designed just for you.

How did you feel at that moment?

Safe? Seen? Cared for?

That's the feeling we strive to create when you walk into a jewellery store. It's not just about viewing ornaments behind glass—it's about stepping into an experience. An invitation to connect. To slow down. To get curious. To fall in love—not just with a piece, but with the story, the craftsmanship, the hands that created it, and the space that welcomes you like a home.

Because when done right, buying jewellery isn't a transaction—it's a celebration.

It is my sincere wish that consumers begin to reclaim the *romance* of the jewellery viewing experience.

And yes—I say *viewing*, not purchasing. Because true jewellery is not something you simply buy; it's something you connect with. It's the stuff of dreams, of memories yet to be made, of self-recognition wrapped in gold and stone.

At our stores, we don't see you as a customer—we see you as a guest. And just as we would in our own home, we want to welcome you with warmth, curiosity, and stories. We want you to ask: *Where did this piece come from? Who made it? What inspired it?* We want to share with you the intricate detailing, the craftsmanship, and the human hand—the *karigar*—whose artistry breathes life into every creation.

Of course, we understand that price matters. Your time is valuable, and your decisions deserve clarity. But if you allow it, the store itself can become part of the magic. Every texture, every display, every sparkle is designed to stir something within you—goosebumps, even—if only you let it.

Because jewellery, at its best, isn't just a product. It's a feeling.

Chapter 2

Jewellery as Emotional Armour

Why We Buy What We Buy?

Jewellery doesn't just sit in a locker or on a neck. It whispers to the world who we are.

- **Some women wear gold like a protective shield**, quietly proud, passed down over generations, a symbol of prudence and preparedness.
- **Others choose to be seen,** in diamonds, sharp, brilliant, impossible to ignore.

Both carry power. But each tells a different story.

Some Brilliant Facts

In 2023 alone, over 2000 tonnes worth of gold jewellery were purchased globally (1 tonne is 1000kg). Not for trend, but for trust. A recent report suggested that across the GCC, **over 65% of women said they consider gold their emergency savings.***

In recent years, the global market for lab-grown diamonds grew by a volume of 38%, driven by a new generation of buyers looking for value, size, and sparkle..

Let's make this more personal.

We've spent time interacting with hundreds of our customers, from homemakers in Karama to the fashionistas of Abu Dhabi. And one thing is clear: **jewellery choices are rarely just about money.**

Amongst many other things, they're about identity.

Let me introduce you to two archetypes:

The Guardian

She buys gold not just for herself, but for her children, for future emergencies, for a legacy.

- Her fears are waste, confusion, and bad timing.
- Her hidden desire? To be respected for her wisdom. To sleep better knowing she's protected.

Take Mrs. M, for instance. She's been buying gold for 20 years.

She doesn't flaunt it, but every piece has a purpose.

She once said, It's not for show. It's for strength.

''If my daughter ever needs financial support, she won't need to knock on banks. All she has to do is open my locker.''

The Dreamer

She wants her jewellery to be seen.

She chooses pieces that shimmer in conversation, that say I've arrived.

- Her fear is being overlooked.
- Her frustration trigger is compromise.
- Her hidden desire? To be remembered, admired, and never mistaken for average.

Take Ms. Z, a corporate lawyer from the UAE. She says—

''If I'm investing in something, it better turn heads. If it doesn't get compliments, why am I even wearing it?"

Of course, most women are a mix of both. But the next time you look at a bracelet or a necklace, pause and ask yourself:

Is this piece armour or spotlight?

Gold and diamonds are not in competition. They are companions in your story. One whispers safety. The other sings ambition.

Your job isn't to choose between them.

It's to choose the right piece for the right moment in your life.

Let's uncover how.

SECTION 2

Traps That Buyers Fall Into

- Making Charges, Misleading Rates & Measurement Myths
- Certificates, Buybacks & Half-Truths
- The Illusion of Variety, Zero Charges & Fast Decisions
- How smart people still lose money—and how to stop

Chapter 3

Understanding Making Charges

Jewellery isn't just about beauty. It's also about clarity.

When you understand how making charges work, you stop being just a buyer.

You become a buyer with power.

Pulling Back the Curtain: What Making Charges Really Mean

Let's pull the curtain back on one of the best-kept secrets in the jewellery industry:

Making charges.

At first glance, the term seems obvious. After all, someone has to make the piece, right? There's labour involved. Design. Setting. Polishing. Finishing. It all adds up.

But what most buyers don't realise is that this—the making charge—is where things often get confusing. Is it too expensive or is it too cheap?

Let's break it down with a real-world example:

Decoding Making Charges

Say the price of gold is 240 AED per gram. You pick up a beautiful 20g bangle. Mathematically, that's 4,800 AED in gold value.

But when your bill arrives, it says 5,760 AED.

Why?

Because an additional 960 AED, about 16%, has been added as a making charge.

This is where many shoppers start to feel uncertain.

- Is this standard?
- Is it inflated?
- Is it even justified?

To answer that, let's trace the journey of that piece of jewellery from its very beginning—from mine to the moment.

The Hidden Chain Behind Every Piece

What you hold in your hand may seem like a simple bangle, but it has passed through at least five different hands before reaching you:

1. **Mined from the earth**: Gold is extracted from quarries, often in remote and harsh environments.
2. **Refined into bars**: The raw gold is sent to refineries, where it is purified and moulded into standardised bars.
3. **Processed into rods or sheets**: These bars are then flattened into rods or sheets using high-pressure machinery.
4. **Transformed into jewellery**: In specialised workshops, the gold is melted (sometimes from old scrap, sometimes new), pressed, cut, wired, and then meticulously crafted.

5. **Sold to wholesalers**, then **distributed to retailers**, before finally making its way to you.

And that's just the supply chain.

The actual creation process is a whole story in itself.

96 to 560 Hours of Creation

After reaching the factory floor, the transformation begins.

The gold, whether bar or scrap, is melted down, then flattened into sheets. These sheets are cut into wires, which are then worked by skilled artisans. At this stage, the karigar begins his magic:

- Grooves are cut into the wire
- Holes are pierced
- Edges are ground down
- Elements are smelted, fused, and shaped into form

This raw creation then passes through **buffing** and **polishing** stages, followed by a **radium dipping** process to bring out its final gleam. Each piece undergoes **rigorous quality checks,** often multiple rounds, before being approved.

From start to finish, a single piece of jewellery can require **anywhere between 96 to 560 hours** of constant, coordinated effort across departments.

More Than a Number: The Art Behind the Price

Here's where most buyers miss the bigger picture:

We've become conditioned to look at jewellery as just weight and price: pure numbers.

But what you're actually wearing is a work of art. A product of heritage, labour, precision, and emotion.

Can you truly reduce the skill of a master karigar, who carves magic out of a plain gold block, to a simple percentage?

Of course, pricing transparency is vital—but so is context.

Making charges isn't just numbers pulled out of thin air.

Think of all of these factors that directly influence making charges :

- Whether it's made by hand or machine
- Whether there is a lot of intricate work involved, which leads to a loss in gold weight due to the etching of the design
- Additional beautification to enhance, like rhodium plating or colour coating, which requires more material and time
- The level of quality check that the piece undergoes
- The ethical and environmental standards of the manufacturer's supply chain
- The purity of the metal, the harder it is (the lower the karat), the more wastage there is in production.

Ultimately, the right perspective is this:

You're not just paying for the gold.

You're paying for the story, the skill, and the soul that went into turning that gold into jewellery you'll treasure for life.

Chapter 4

Third-Party Certificates Guarantee Diamond Quality?

The Hidden Truth About Diamond Certification

When it comes to diamonds, most buyers understandably place a lot of faith in certification. And yes, certification is progress—it offers a structured way to **evaluate stones based on the 4Cs: Cut, Colour, Clarity, and Carat.**

But here's what many people don't know:

There are dozens of diamond grading labs around the world, each with different standards, reputations, and commercial motives. **Not all certifications are created equal**. Some labs are globally recognised **while others operate on looser parameters that may skew in favour of the seller.**

And even within those certifications, critical visual cues are missing.

Did you know that certified diamond jewellery does not mention visible "tinges"—such as a faint grey, brown, or green hue—that can drastically dull the appearance of your stone? (Some labs mention this as 'BGM', but it's fairly cryptic, and I am yet to meet a consumer who understands what those letters mean.)

That's right. A diamond may appear cloudy or lifeless under natural light and still receive a perfectly acceptable grading on paper. Worse still, once a diamond is set into a piece of jewellery, inclusions that were previously visible can be hidden in the pavilion (the bottom side of the diamond), escaping all scrutiny unless the stone is removed and re-examined.

So, while certification is an important starting point, it's not the final word.

What's Really Under the Hood?

When you're buying a diamond set in jewellery, you're often buying blind. Why? Because what's "under the hood" can make a big difference, and yet most buyers don't even know what to ask.

Here are a few lesser-known but critical factors:

Girdle Inclusions: Inclusions located on the girdle (the side edge of the diamond) may be entirely hidden once the stone is mounted, **making the diamond appear cleaner than it really is.**

Fat Girdles: Some diamonds carry disproportionate weight in the girdle. This adds to the carat weight (and the price), but not to the face-up size. **The result? You pay more for a diamond that looks smaller than its weight suggests.**

Ask your jeweller whether they do this kind of quality assessment at the production stage or not. Accordingly, make your decisions.

Carat ≠ Size: Carat measures weight, not visual diameter. A poorly proportioned 1-carat diamond can appear smaller than a well-cut 0.85-carat diamond, and still cost more.

The Price You Don't See

Diamond pricing isn't linear—it's **exponential**. For example, if a well-cut 1-carat diamond is priced at **18,500 AED**, a 2-carat diamond of similar quality might cost **55,000 AED** or more.

This pricing is guided by the **Rapaport Price List**, a global benchmark that maps diamond values across weight, colour and clarity brackets. Some buyers often look for diamonds just *below* the next size tier—for example, a **1.90 ct instead of a full 2.00 ct–to get almost the same visual impact at a significantly better price.**

Here's how that looks in real terms:

- **A 2.00 ct round diamond** may be listed at **55,000 AED**.
- **A 1.90 ct diamond** with similar quality and cut might cost only **49,000 AED**.
- Visually? Almost identical. Financially? **A saving of 6,000 AED**.

To the naked eye, the difference in size is nearly impossible to spot—but your bank account will feel the difference.

Liquid or Illiquid? The Resale Reality

Diamonds can be resold, but they may often be illiquid assets, especially high-value solitaires. It may take time to find a buyer, and the resale value is often substantially lower than the purchase price. This can feel disheartening if you're expecting quick liquidity.

That's why many buyers are better off choosing jewellers with clear, transparent trade-in or upgrade policies. But even here, caution is advised—some retailers bury exclusions and confusing clauses in fine print.

Always ask:

- "What will you offer me if I return this in two years?"
- Get it in writing. Don't accept vague promises.

Diamonds as Luxury, Not Investment

Unlike gold, which has global liquidity, uniform purity standards, and steady value appreciation, diamonds are luxury items first and foremost. Their value is subjective, perception-driven, and often inflated by branding and presentation.

They are status symbols first, savings instruments second. And that's okay, if you see them as such.

So buy that diamond. Wear it. Celebrate it. Let it mark a milestone in your life. But **be clear on what it is: a symbol of style and success, not your proof of prudence or your ability to invest in financial assets.**

Over time, as you move up in life, trade in your status symbols for new ones. Upgrade, evolve, reinvent, and always ask the questions that keep your jeweller honest.

Because in diamonds, as in life, clarity is everything.

Chapter 5

The Illusion of 'Zero Making Charges'

You've heard the phrase: "All that glitters is not gold."

It's especially true today. The jewellery industry has changed. Healthy competition has created a market where customers often walk away with great deals, and that's a win.

In places like India, initiatives like hallmarking now ensure buyers get the purity they pay for. And in my residing country in the UAE (where there has been very strict government control ensuring purity standards are met), retailers follow a unified board price for gold, giving everyone a clear and transparent starting point.

But when it comes to making charges (as touched upon briefly in the previous chapter, also), things get murkier.

Some retailers charge higher making fees, others lower.

And then came a marketing masterstroke—"Zero making charges."

On the surface, it sounds like a bargain: you get your jewellery, and the seller makes nothing on labour.

But here's the catch: Someone still has to pay the *karigar*—the artisan who actually makes your jewellery.

So if the store isn't charging you, either:

- The work has been mass-produced, often at the cost of detail and quality, giving you an inferior quality product.
- Or the price is hidden elsewhere, just wearing a different label

Let's take a moment to understand the real story behind a piece of jewellery.

The Hands Behind the Sparkle

Jewellery doesn't come out of a machine with a bow on it. It begins as a plain gold bar. It's melted, rolled, cut, wired, shaped, carved, polished, dipped, checked—and then checked again.

And at the heart of this process is the *karigar*—a craftsman using traditional tools, muscle memory, and immense skill. He doesn't just make a product. He sculpts emotion into metal, like a master sculptor chiselling art from stone.

When I take people into our factory, **they're stunned. Not just by the number of steps, but by the human effort involved.** Each piece travels through many hands and many hours, often over a hundred.

So What Does 'Zero Charges' Really Mean?

When someone says **"zero making charge," it might seem like a deal—but it's a bit of a trick.**

You're not comparing apples to apples.

Would you compare:

A handcrafted, hand-polished piece created over 120 hours...

With a mass-produced item that rolls off a machine in minutes?

It's unfair to the artisan. And it's unfair to you, the buyer, if you think both are the same.

The making charge isn't just a cost—it's respect. It's how we value the time, effort, and legacy of the people behind the product.

What Discerning Buyers Should Know

If you see jewellery as part of your life's story, as something meaningful, symbolic, or emotional, then it deserves to be crafted, not churned.

A karigar's time, skill, and pride deserve to be honoured, not erased with a price tag that says "zero."

So next time you're offered a deal that sounds too good to be true, ask yourself:

Is this just gold I'm buying? Or is it something more meaningful to me?

Because jewellery should never be priced like a commodity—it should be valued like a memory.

Chapter 6

The Illusion of Variety

The Illusion of New: What Jewellery Stores Don't Tell You

Walk into a jewellery showroom and you're likely to hear—

- "This just came in."
- The displays look refreshed.
- Designs seem new.
- You assume you're seeing the latest trends, hot off the bench.

But here's the reality:

Many large retailers rotate non-selling stock between branches to give the *illusion* of freshness.

It's a clever merchandising tactic, and it works.

This doesn't mean they're being dishonest. It's just how the retail engine runs.

The Hidden Cycle of Jewellery Procurement

The process of curating jewellery is both **a science and an art**. Retailers spend months tracking trends, analysing data, and collaborating with vendors to create pieces they believe will resonate with consumers.

But here's the shift most buyers don't see:

The **core categories** of jewellery, like gold bangles, solitaire rings, bridal sets, or daily wear pendants, **don't change dramatically**. Instead, **what sells well is** quietly **repeated**, and **what doesn't is moved around**.

It's just like fashion retail.

Walk into any premium clothing store and you'll always find a **black T-shirt in medium size**. It may be folded differently or hung on another rack, but it's the same essential piece, because it *sells*. Retailers restock what works, then layer on fresh colours, embellishments, or cuts to keep things visually exciting.

Jewellery follows the same rule.

Understanding the "New Arrival" Myth

Design trends in jewellery **do evolve, but far more slowly than social media would have you believe.**

On average, true shifts in consumer taste or design language take 2–3 years to develop.

So while you may hear about "new collections" every few months, much of what's shown is a **variation of a core classic**, not a complete reinvention.

Retailers know that consumers crave novelty.

So instead of constantly designing from scratch, they rely on:

- Rotating old stock across showrooms
- Re-packaging bestsellers in limited edition finishes
- Introducing seasonal themes using existing moulds

This creates a steady rhythm of "what's new"—without actually reinventing the wheel.

How to Spot What's *Actually* New

If you're genuinely curious about the latest designs, **skip the display cases** and ask for the retailer's **catalogue or lookbook**.

These curated previews usually contain:

- Their newest pieces, fresh from production
- The designs they're most proud of
- Limited editions or seasonal launches

These are the collections that *do* reflect current innovation, often incorporating newer techniques, gemstones, or cultural themes.

A Smarter Way to Shop

The key takeaway?

Not every new display means a new design.

True jewellery classics like traditional 22K bangles, solitaire studs, or gold chains *never really go out of style*. What changes is how they're merchandised, framed, and marketed.

So next time you're browsing a store and something feels familiar, trust your instinct. It probably is.

And remember: in jewellery, **timelessness often matters more than trendiness.** Choose what speaks to you, not just what's placed under a spotlight.

Chapter 7

The Smart Buyer Checklist

If you read only one section of this book, let it be this one.

Because these are the **exact mistakes we see smart, educated buyers make every single day**. Not because they're careless, but because no one ever told them *what to ask*.

The jewellery industry, for all its beauty, often hides important truths behind shiny lights and fast-talking sales pitches. But buying jewellery doesn't have to feel like guesswork or a gamble.

This checklist is designed to help you:

- Shop with clarity, not confusion
- Ask the right questions before parting with your money
- Avoid emotional regret and maximise long-term value
- Feel *in control*—not just impressed—when you walk into a showroom

These six insights aren't technical jargon or complex calculations. They're simple, powerful shifts that can **transform you from a passive buyer into a confident decision-maker**.

Mistake 1: Ignoring the Making Charges

This is one of the most overlooked ways buyers lose money, without even realising it.

You ask for the gold rate. You do a quick mental calculation. You think you've figured out the price.

But wait—what about the *making charge*?

The making charge is the cost of turning raw gold into a wearable piece. It covers labour, design, setting, finishing, and the artistry behind it. But many jewellers mention it casually, or not at all, leaving you with an inflated final bill you didn't see coming.

Here's a simple rule of thumb:

- For **plain gold jewellery**, a **3%–15%** making charge is considered standard.
- **Anything higher?** *Ask why.*

Is the piece more intricate? Is it a designer collection? Or are you simply being overcharged?

Knowing this doesn't just save you money. It ensures you're paying *fairly* for the craftsmanship, not unknowingly funding inflated markups.

Mistake 2: Buying Diamonds Without Clarity on the 4Cs

Cut. Colour. Clarity. Carat.

These four factors, known as the 4Cs, determine both the beauty *and* value of a diamond.

Yet, surprisingly, many buyers don't fully understand them, and that's exactly where poor decisions happen.

If you're not crystal clear on the 4Cs, you're essentially **relying entirely on the salesperson's pitch**, instead of your own judgment.

Here's how to protect yourself:

- **Insist on certification** from a respected lab. Don't accept vague paperwork.

- **Ask to see the diamond under magnification**—a reputable store will always accommodate this.
- **Trust your eyes.** Does the diamond sparkle cleanly? Is the tint visible? Do the inclusions bother *you*?

Remember: a high carat weight doesn't always mean a better diamond. A poorly cut 1-carat stone can look smaller and duller than a well-cut 0.80-carat one.

Without a clear understanding of the 4Cs, you may end up overpaying, or worse, taking home a diamond that doesn't truly shine.

Mistake 3: Assuming All Gold Is 21K or 22K—And Everything Else Is Inferior

Many buyers walk into a store believing that **only 21K or 22K gold is "real" gold**, and anything less—like 18K or 14K—is substandard.

That's simply not true.

Yes, 22K gold is more pure—containing about **91.6% pure gold**—and it's traditionally used in classic jewellery, especially in Indian and Middle Eastern markets. But **purity doesn't always mean practicality**.

For pieces with delicate, detailed designs—like filigree, fine settings, or jewellery with sharp edges—18K or even 14K gold is often preferred.

Why? Because it's **stronger and more durable**, thanks to its alloy mix.

A **well-crafted 18K piece from a reputable jeweller isn't "lesser"**—it's just **better suited for the design**.

What matters is **transparency**.

Make sure you're:

- Told exactly what karat purity you're buying
- Paying the correct rate for that purity
- Aware of why a piece is made in 18K or 14K

Don't judge a piece only by the karat stamp; judge it by whether it's **fit for the purpose**, and **whether the jeweller is honest** about why it was made that way.

Mistake 4: Not Checking the Buyback Policy

Jewellery is often seen as both a treasure and a form of wealth. But what happens when you want to return, upgrade, or exchange it?

Most buyers forget to ask this one crucial question **before** they purchase:

> ***"If I come back in two years, what will you offer me?"***

And the answers can vary *wildly*.

- Some jewellers offer **100% value on gold weight**, but deduct the **making charges**.
- Others offer partial refunds on **diamond jewellery**, sometimes **40-70% or less**.
- A few **may have unclear or confusing terms buried in their paperwork**, making it hard to claim fair value later.

Here's the truth: Your exit strategy matters just as much as your entry.

Always ask:

- How much will I get back on gold?
- What happens with diamonds or coloured stones?

- Is the buyback value fixed or at the market rate?
- Will I get it in cash or only as store credit?

Knowing this upfront won't just protect your investment, it will give you **peace of mind**

Mistake 5: Being Lured by Discounts Instead of Quality

A shiny **"30% OFF"** tag can feel like a win, but in many cases, it's just clever marketing.

Here's the inside truth: that discount is often **already priced in**.

It may come from:

- Inflated making charges
- Older or slow-moving inventory
- Or simply an artificially marked-up MRP (maximum retail price) designed to make the "discount" look appealing

Real value isn't in a discount: it's in **craftsmanship, durability, and integrity**.

Choose jewellery that's well-made, fairly priced, and beautiful enough to be worn for years, not just something that seemed like a "steal" at the moment.

A timeless piece that *lasts and gleams* will always be worth more than a flashy deal that fades with time.

Mistake 6: Not Asking: "Is This Piece Me?"

Too often, buyers choose jewellery based on what they think they *should* buy, what's trending, what others admire, or what feels "safe."

But jewellery isn't just decoration. It's self-expression.

Every piece you wear should reflect **your energy, your lifestyle, and your story**. It should feel like *you*, not just something that looks good in a box.

Before you commit, ask yourself:

- Does this piece excite me?
- Can I see myself wearing it often?
- Does it feel effortless, or forced?

Don't buy for others. Buy for the person in the mirror.

Because when jewellery is chosen with authenticity, it doesn't just sparkle, it *speaks*.

SECTION 3

Planning Like a Pro

How to shop with clarity: by occasion, moment, and mindset

- Gold vs Diamond – What's Right for This Season of Your Life?
- Timing Your Purchase Smartly (Festivals, SIPs, and Life Events)

The Cheat Sheet

When to Buy, What to Gift, and How to Plan Ahead

Chapter 8

Gold Vs Diamond

What About Lab-Grown Diamonds?

- "Are they real?"
- "Are they worth it?"
- "Are they fake?"

These are the questions we hear often, and understandably so. There's still some debate in the minds of many buyers.

So let's clear the air with the plain truth:

Lab-grown diamonds are real diamonds.

They are chemically, physically, and optically identical to mined diamonds. The difference? Instead of forming below the Earth over millions of years, they're grown in advanced laboratories above the ground, using highly controlled environments that replicate natural processes.

They are not to be confused with simulants like zircon, moissanite, or cubic zirconia. Those are imitation stones that merely look like diamonds.

Lab-grown diamonds are diamonds, just with a different origin story.

They're produced in large quantities and, just as importantly, consumed in large quantities too.

Are They a Good Investment?

If by investment you mean something that will increase in monetary value over time, the honest answer is: No.

Lab-grown diamonds do not appreciate in resale value the way traditional commodities like gold might. In fact, most jewellery in general, especially diamond-set jewellery, is not designed for short-term financial gain.

But that doesn't mean lab-grown diamonds aren't worth it.

Let's rethink the word investment.

You buy a luxury car. The smell of the leather, the feel of the wheel, the thrill of admiration as it glides out of the showroom—all of it is part of the experience. You know the car won't gain value. But you didn't buy it for that. You bought it for the feeling.

Jewellery works the same way.

Lab-grown diamonds, in particular, offer you the chance to own a larger, clearer, and more brilliant stone at a fraction of the cost of a mined diamond. The size and sparkle are undeniable. And yes, it will turn heads. People will notice. Compliments will come.

So when someone says, "Wow, what a stunning diamond, looks amazing on you,"

ask yourself:

Isn't that a return worth investing in?

Lab-grown diamonds are not just cost-effective alternatives.

They are emotionally rewarding, status-enhancing, and style-defining expressions of modern luxury.

And that, too, is valuable.

Gold vs Diamond? Which is the Smarter Buy Right Now?

If you've ever stood in a jewellery store, torn between a glittering diamond necklace in one showcase and a bold gold set in another, you've faced the timeless question:

Which one makes more sense? Emotionally? Financially? Practically?

Let's break it down.

The Emotional ROI

Gold whispers safety. Diamonds shout status.

Gold is thoughtful; it's what you buy with your family in mind. It carries tradition, becomes an heirloom, and brings a quiet sense of security. It's the jewellery you imagine passing on.

Diamonds, on the other hand, are bold. They're about *you.* They turn heads. They're made for the moments where you want to be seen, to shine, to leave a lasting impression.

So ask yourself:

> ***Are you buying for the next celebration—***
> ***or the next generation?***

The Financial Return

Gold holds value.

Let's not sugarcoat it.

Over the past 20 years, gold has appreciated by nearly 500%. It's globally recognised, easily liquidated, and widely understood. It's not just a purchase—it's a financial safety net.

Diamonds? Particularly mined diamonds tend to **depreciate** the moment you walk out of the store, unless you're buying ultra-rare, investment-grade stones (and most people aren't). That being said, over the long term, they have held onto their value and can therefore be called an effective store of value.

But here's the twist.

Lab-grown diamonds cost 60–80% less than their mined counterparts and deliver *emotional ROI* that's sky-high. You get the sparkle, the size, the admiration—without burning through your savings.

So, eventually we come back to the fact that it's your choice!

The Resale Reality

Gold is gold.

If it's 22K, its value is pegged to the global market. You can sell it, pawn it, or pass it down. Jewellers will buy it back. Banks understand it. Families protect it.

Diamonds? That's where things get tricky.

Even high-quality stones may fetch only a fraction of what you paid—unless you're working with a jeweller who offers strong buyback or upgrade programs. Without that, resale can be frustrating and slow.

So, What's the *Real* Smart Choice?

It's not about choosing one over the other.

The smartest buyers know this:

Buy with intention.

- **Starting out?** Build your base with 22K or 21K plain gold; it's a savings plan in disguise.
- **Celebrating something special?** Treat yourself to lab-grown or mined diamonds, because special moments deserve a splash of luxury.
- **Thinking long-term?** Blend both. Own timeless gold staples *and* a diamond piece that lights you up every time you wear it.

Let your locker hold your legacy.

Let your necklace light up the room.

One whispers. The other sings.

Both belong to you.

Smart Jewellery Buying: Gold vs. Mined vs. Lab-Grown Diamonds

Factor	22K Gold Jewellery	Mined Diamonds	Lab-Grown Diamonds
Emotional Value	Symbol of tradition, family, and security	Statement of status, luxury, and elegance	Bold self-expression, modern luxury, high impact
Financial Value	Appreciates over time, globally liquid	Depreciates after purchase (unless investment-grade) long-term holds value	Lower cost, but not a financial investment

Resale/ Buyback	High resale value, accepted worldwide	Low resale unless backed by a jeweller's exchange policy	Resale value is currently limited, and trade-in options vary
Cost to Buy	Medium (depends on weight and purity)	High (premium pricing per carat)	Lower cost than mined
Visual Impact	Subtle, timeless, classic glow	Brilliant sparkle, prestige-based appeal	Larger, cleaner stones at the same price point
Best For	Long-term savings, heirloom pieces	Milestones, weddings, special gifts	Eye-catching looks, celebrations, and personal treats
Purity/ Authenticity	91.6% pure (22K), 87.5% (21K) verified by hallmark	100% diamond, naturally formed	100% diamond, lab-grown but chemically identical
Cultural Meaning	Deep-rooted in tradition, rituals, and heritage	Modern luxury, status-focused	Emerging symbol of innovation, conscious luxury

Chapter 9

When to Buy - Timing Your Jewellery Purchase Smartly

Timing isn't just for the stock market. It matters in jewellery too.

One of the most common questions I hear, almost reflexively, the moment someone finds out what I do, is:

"Gold's at an all-time high.
Should I buy now or wait?"

My answer usually makes people pause:

"Well, I'm in the 'feeling good' and 'love' business...
not the ROI business."

Because jewellery isn't just about price. It's about emotion, identity, and life's biggest moments. But I understand where the question comes from, especially when the gold rate dominates headlines.

Let's explore the reality behind the rate and how smart buyers *actually* time their purchases.

Gold Rates: Myth vs. Reality

Here's something that might surprise you:

Most jewellers don't profit when gold rates rise.

We've been in the gold jewellery trade since it was $100 **an ounce**—today, it's pushing **$3300 an ounce**. And yet, our margins haven't magically multiplied.

Why? **Because we're not speculators.** We're not in the gold price trading business. **We're in the service business, crafting memories, not playing the markets.**

Still, it's a common myth: that rising gold prices mean fatter profits for jewellers. In truth, we adjust daily to the global gold rate, and what we earn is from our craftsmanship and service, not the gold price itself.

The Problem With Timing the Market

If you're constantly trying to time the bottom, you may end up sitting on the sidelines forever.

Gold dips, when they happen, are often short-lived. You may see a **10–30 AED** drop per gram, but if you hesitate, that window may close before you act.

That's why **smart buyers don't chase the rate. They focus on the right time for them.**

A Better Strategy: Time the *Moments*

Here's what savvy jewellery buyers do instead:

- **Festive seasons** like **Diwali, Eid**, or **Akshaya Tritiya** often bring great offers, but also *massive crowds*. If you want selection, shop **early** before the rush begins.

- **Off-season months** like **May–June** or **January** (after the holiday spike) tend to be quieter. You'll find better negotiation power, more relaxed service, and sometimes hidden gems in stock.
- **Gold rate dips** don't come often, but when they do, consider **locking in with a small advance**. Most jewellers allow you to secure the rate with partial payment and design selection later.
- **Life moments** like birthdays, anniversaries, job promotions, or personal milestones are also perfect occasions to buy. Jewellery bought during these times carries deeper meaning—it becomes a marker, not just a material.

A Real Story:
The Power of Small, Consistent Action

One of our senior team members shared a story that stuck with me.

A regular customer once walked into our store, looking visibly anxious. When asked, he admitted he was worried about the future; he had two young daughters and was concerned about the rising cost of living, especially the tradition of gifting gold at weddings.

The advice he received?

"Just start saving 300 AED a month in Gold Saving Plans. Small steps. No pressure."

He followed that advice.

Fifteen years later, that small monthly habit funded both weddings, with no financial stress.

Gold didn't just store value—it created security, joy, and dignity.

Pro Tips From the Pros

- **Client R** always books her **wedding season jewellery in July**, well before the rush. She gets first access to new designs, better service, and locks in her rate before seasonal spikes.
- **Consistency beats timing.** Whether it's saving monthly or watching the market without obsession, it's your *discipline*, not luck, that creates value.
- **Plan for events, not prices.** Jewellery isn't a commodity to flip. It's a *story* you wear. So make sure the *timing* adds to the *meaning*.

How to Time Your Purchase Smartly

When?	Why It Works!
Festive Pre-Season (1–2 months before)	Wider selection, early offers, calm service experience
Off-Season Months (May–June, Jan)	Better negotiation, more attention from staff
On Small Gold Rate Dips (10–15 AED)	Great time to lock in a rate with an advance payment
Milestones & Life Events	Emotional value enhances the purchase more than timing ever will
Monthly Gold Savings Plans	Builds wealth steadily in a stress-free manner.

So, should you buy now?

That depends.

But one thing is clear:

The best time to buy jewellery is when it means something.

Not when it's trending. Not when it's cheapest.

When it's *right for you.*

SECTION 4

The Final Touch

Confidence. Customisation. Care.

- The Finer Details That Make All The Difference
- Gifting Jewellery: Not Just Metal, Core Memories
- Jewellery For Men: The Quiet Power Move
- Before You Leave the Store – Your Final Buyer Promise

Note to Self
"My Next Jewellery Decision Will Be…"

Chapter 10

It's All In The Details

Let's face it, no one ever cried over an investment portfolio (unless it tanked). But they have cried over a necklace. Especially when it comes with a clasp that just won't open on the day of the wedding, that's where 'the final touch' comes in.

Jewellery may be sold in grams, but its true weight is in the details, details that live in the quiet, quirky corners of our workshops. Where karigars, those mystical beings in faded kurtas and untamed eyebrows, sit cross-legged, doing things with tools so tiny, they might as well be fixing watches for ants.

You don't see these men (and sometimes women), but your jewellery does. Every edge they smooth, every claw they tighten, every last polishing cloth they whisper secrets to—it all shows up when you walk into a room and someone says, 'Wow, that piece is something else.'

Let's pause and honour the unsung heroes who've permanently bonded their fingerprints to your ring. The karigar who stayed ten minutes longer just to re-align the pendant you'd never notice was slightly off-centre. These people are artists, therapists, engineers, and low-key miracle workers rolled into one.

Now, before you walk out of any jewellery store, here are a few underrated rituals that are part of the 'final touch'—the ones that take your piece from 'purchased' to 'precious.'

These are five essential checks that combine practicality, comfort, and respect for the artistry behind what you wear.

1. **The Clasp Test**

   Because security is style's quiet companion.

   Before purchasing any chain, pendant, or bracelet, test the clasp. Fasten and unfasten it yourself, not just once, but a few times. It should feel smooth but secure. If it's too tight, it may strain the piece over time. Too loose, and you risk losing it. A secure clasp is what allows you to wear your piece with confidence, not fear.

2. **The Finger Wiggle Test**

   Because a ring should fit your finger, not fight it.

   Slip the ring on and gently wiggle your finger. It should glide on with a little resistance and come off without force. If it slides off too easily, you may lose it. If it's too tight, you'll hesitate to wear it.

3. **The Hair-Snag Check**

   Comfort is elegance in disguise.

   Run your fingers through your hair while wearing the earrings. If they catch or pull, the setting may have sharp edges or raised prongs that need refining. Jewellery shouldn't demand discomfort to look good. The best pieces disappear into your lifestyle, not into your hair.

4. **The Mirror Moment**

   Because how you look & feel matters more than how it looks on the shelf.

   Stand in front of the mirror– Yes, we get it, you are admiring yourself (rightly so) on the pretext of inspecting the piece.

Do your eyes light up? Do your shoulders lift just a little? Jewellery should enhance your presence, not overpower it. The moment you wear something and *feel like yourself, elevated,* that's when you know it's right.

5. **Gratitude For The Karigar's Blessing**

   Because behind every piece is a pair of hands—and a legacy.

   Take a moment to appreciate the invisible touch behind your jewellery: the hands of the *karigar*, the skilled artisan who shaped, carved, polished, and perfected your piece. Their touch is not mechanical; it carries tradition, discipline, and quiet pride. Though unseen, their fingerprints remain in every detail. Some say a karigar's touch brings good luck. We believe it brings something even deeper: the soul.

Wear it with gratitude.

Jewellery isn't mass-produced magic. It's deliberate. It's personal. It's the soft chime of effort, creativity, and care coming together to say, 'Here, this is for you.'

So yes, you can know the 4Cs, ask for the hallmark, compare prices, and still miss the best part—the art that happens when no one's watching.

That, my friend, is the final touch.
And it's what turns gold into grace.

Chapter 11

Gifting Jewellery
Not Metal, But Memories

There's a big difference between gifting jewellery and gifting joy.

Jewellery becomes truly meaningful when it carries emotion, thought, and story. If you want your gift to be remembered forever, here's how to make it unforgettable:

1. **Know Their Style**

   Before you buy, ask yourself:

   Are they classic or modern? Bold or minimal? Do they love gold or prefer diamonds? Choosing something that reflects *them* shows you've paid attention—and that matters.

2. **Add a Personal Touch**

   Engrave a name, a special date, or even a small symbol. A subtle detail can turn a beautiful piece into something deeply personal.

3. **Tell the Story**

   Include a short note or message explaining *why* you chose this piece. Maybe it reminds you of a moment you shared, or a quality you admire. That small story adds emotional weight far beyond the piece itself.

4. **Presentation Matters**

   Don't overlook the wrapping. Elegant, thoughtful packaging makes the moment feel luxurious and memorable, before the box is even opened.

5. **It's Not About the Price**

   Don't focus on how much you spent. Focus on what it means.

One young man gifted his fiancée a simple pendant, woven with their initials. She cried.

Not because it was expensive.

Because it was intimate. Thoughtful. Timeless.

Gifting jewellery isn't about budget, it's about **emotion**.

Do it with care, and you won't just give them something to wear.

You'll give them something they'll *never forget.*

Chapter 12

Jewellery for Men? The Quiet Power Move

It's no longer just about watches and cufflinks.

Today's man wears jewellery that says he's arrived, without saying a word.

- A simple 22k gold chain under the shirt.
- A subtle diamond stud worn only on special evenings.
- A platinum ring with his family crest.

Men's jewellery is rising, and it's not just a trend. It's a return to heritage.

From South Indian grooms proudly wearing thick kasu malas to Gulf businessmen choosing engraved cuff bangles made in platinum, it's about identity and quiet strength.

A client, Mr. K, once said, I don't speak much at events. But my ring does.

If you're buying for your husband, brother, or son, choose something timeless. **Jewellery for men is not about being flashy. It's about being unforgettable.**

Chapter 13

From Buyer to Believer

If you've made it this far, you're not just looking to buy jewellery.

You're looking to buy better.

You've seen the fine print. You've decoded the myths. You've stepped beyond sales pitches into smart, soulful choices.

You are now what most jewellers call a rare buyer. Someone who values emotion and education equally.

You know that gold isn't just about karats. Diamonds aren't just about sparkle.

And jewellery isn't just about adornment.

It's about becoming.

- Becoming the woman whose necklace starts conversations.
- The daughter whose bangles hold stories.
- The bride whose diamonds shine with purpose.
- The buyer who never regrets her choice.

We're honoured to have shared this journey with you.

Because in a world full of quick buys and forgettable trends, you chose to pause. To learn. To care.

You chose not just jewellery, but meaning.

That makes you unforgettable.

Here's to your next piece, not just being worn, but *lived in.*

A memory in the making. A legacy in gold.

Thank you for letting us be part of your story.

Let this be the beginning, not the end? of how you buy.

Stay curious. Stay powerful.

And above all, stay unforgettable.

Your Next Step — Be Someone's Spark

If this book gave you even one new insight…

If it made you pause, smile, or see jewellery differently…

Don't keep it to yourself.

Share it with a friend. A daughter. A colleague.

Someone who deserves to buy with clarity, confidence, and joy.

Because the most precious things we pass on aren't just gold or diamonds, they're wisdom.

And that makes you the real jeweller now.

Authentically Yours,

Rohan Siroya

CEO Retail, Siroya Jewellers, CEO Evermore Diamonds

Est. 1992| Stores across Dubai, U.A.E.

Website: www.siroya.com

Instagram: @siroyajewellers